Family Prayers

Nick Aiken
&
Rowan Williams

Paulist Press
New York/Mahwah, New Jersey

First published in Great Britain in 2002 by
SPCK, Holy Trinity Church, Marylebone Road,
London NW1 4DU

Text copyright © Nick Aiken and Rowan Williams 2002
This edition copyright © The Society for Promoting Christian Knowledge 2002

ISBN: 0-8091-0550-0

Published in North America in 2002 by
Paulist Press
997 Macarthur Boulevard
Mahwah, New Jersey 07430

www.paulistpress.com

Designed and produced by Tony Cantale Graphics

Printed in Singapore

$\mathcal{C}$ontents

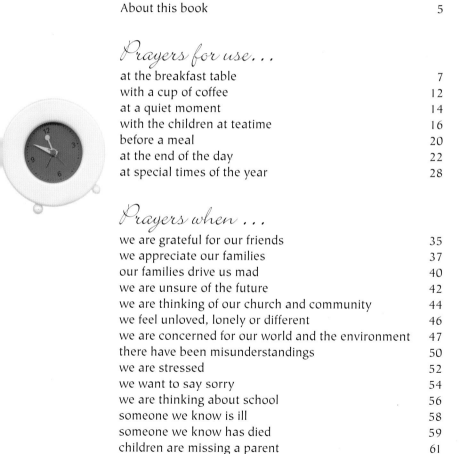

Acknowledgements

*I*WOULD like to express a huge thank you to Pyrford Church of England Primary School for their involvement in *Family Prayers*. Many of the children contributed to this book so that their prayers might benefit other families. Also I would like to thank the parishioners of Wisley and Pyrford for being such a great bunch of people and offering their encouragement. And finally I would like to thank Rowan Williams, who gave me the original idea for *Family Prayers* and who has worked closely with me on its production.

We are also very pleased to give all the royalties from *Family Prayers* to The Children's Society to support their vital work.

Nick Aiken
Pyrford, Woking, Surrey

Making it work for you

Prayer is not easy, and it's even more difficult if you are trying to pray as a family because there are so many distractions. Our most common prayer time together is at the front door, trying to get our two boys off to school on time. Hilary or I usually say, 'Thank you for today', and the boys respond, 'Amen'. We then open the door and head towards school hoping to get there before the bell goes. We are not always successful.

You may be one of those families who live calm, well-ordered lives and are always in control – in which case you are the exception. Family life makes a lot of demands and it's not easy to find the space and opportunity to fit prayer in. So make it work for you, and don't think it has to be done in a certain way. Just be natural about it. The best time may be around the breakfast table for a minute or just a few seconds in the morning. It may be at the front door just before going off to school. Or with the evening meal, or at bedtime. Whatever time suits you as a family is okay.

It would be nice to say family prayers every day. Sometimes we may manage it, but often with children the unexpected intervenes and some mishap shatters the calm. So go for what is possible. If you as a family can manage it realistically only at weekends, then go with that. Please don't regard that as a failure, because it's not.

What's your style?

In this book we provide a variety of styles of prayer. Some are very casual and conversational in their manner; after all it was one of the saints, Clement of Alexandria, who said, 'Prayer is conversation with God.' And maybe that's the style you and your family naturally take to.

On the other hand, we have also woven in prayers involving several family members in a more formal and ordered manner. One style is not better than the other; they are just different aspects of what prayer is about. Don't be put off by something that is not your style. Use the prayers that suit you, and if you prefer one style over another then that is fine.

Making it easier

If you have managed to achieve a few moments together as a family to pray, you may like to make it more effective by adding something to the occasion, like lighting a candle. Of course, if your children are too young this could be a recipe for disaster, but if they are old enough, lighting a candle is a simple way of marking out a brief but special time. Even if your children don't understand the meaning of all that is being said, they will sense something of the occasion through the gentle candle-light and the feeling of the moment.

Or you could use a picture. This could be something the children have previously done themselves at church or school, particularly if it has a Christian meaning. It can then act as a focus for you praying together. You could also use a cross, placing it on a table in the centre, helping every member of the family understand who it is we are praying to.

These are just a few simple suggestions. I'm sure you could think of other items that could be used. Experiment, and see what helps you.

Enjoy using this book

We hope that you enjoy using *Family Prayers*, with the variety of styles of prayer and the range of everyday matters we touch on. But what we offer here is not in any way the limit. Indeed, we hope this book may be just a stepping-stone for you towards creating your own family prayers and spiritual activities you can do together. In fact, it would be great to know what styles of prayer work for you, and to be able to share that with other families. Write to us, care of Triangle – we would love to hear from you.

Prayers for use at the breakfast table

These prayers can be said by any member of the family on behalf of everyone else. However, some have suggestions as to who might say different sections; use or adapt these ideas according to who is taking part at the time.

Lord, thank you for today.
Amen.

Lord, guide, help and protect us throughout this day. Amen.

Lord, in all the things we have got to do today, please be with us. Amen.

ALL:

Lord, your beauty fills the earth and the sky;
    the saints and angels sing to you,
God everlasting, Father, Son and Holy Spirit.

MOM:

Let's keep quiet in God's company.
As we breathe in and out, we think
of God's Spirit, God's breath,
keeping all the world alive.

Silence for about a minute.

7

DAD:

Listen to what God tells us in the Bible.

*Dad or another member of the family reads Psalm 34.1–10
or the next paragraph of the Bible passage the family is
reading. You might choose to do this with St Mark's Gospel.
It's the shortest, and children will easily recognize the stories.*

ALL:

Amen.

Dear God, thank you for another day.
Thank you for my family and friends.
Help us today to think about other people
and not just about ourselves.
Amen.

SON OR DAUGHTER:

It's time to praise God for who he is and
what he does!

ALL:

How wonderful,
how beautiful you are;
the whole world sings to you,
the everliving Father.

MOM OR DAD:

In heaven the angels worship you;
your friends and followers worship you;
all who risked their lives for your sake
worship you.

SON OR DAUGHTER:

It's time to think about people who need
praying for!

> *A short period for naming people or
> situations needing prayer.*

MOM OR DAD:

Let's say together the Lord's Prayer.
Our Father…

> *All join in.*

SON OR DAUGHTER:

Dear God, thank you for a new day;
thank you for the rest we've had in the night.
Help us today to keep away from all that's wrong,
and live the way you made us to live;
for Jesus' sake.
Amen.

Lord, open my eyes to the needs of others,
that by word or deed,
I may be their friend today.
Amen.

Lord, we thank you that we live so comfortably.
Our food is always hot and there is plenty.
We have our own rooms, with soft warm beds
and wonderful toys.
It's great to have our TV and computers and
stereo.
We thank you that our lives are so far from
danger and hard times.
Please help us remember to be grateful every
day,
and to show our thanks by being generous with
all that we have:
our money, our food, our time, our smiles, our
interest in others.
We pray these things in your name.
Amen.

Dear Lord, as we pray,
the sun starts a different day.
The morning gathers its great look,
opening like the pages of a book!

Prayers for use with a cup of coffee

Lord, it's another day. The kids have gone to school, my partner is at work and the house is filthy, and there is so much going on in my life that often I do not have time to know what I think or feel. But I want you to know that I'm here, so keep an eye on me. Thanks.

Dear God, thank you for this coffee I am now going to drink, because it has been through a lot of trouble. It has been grown in Africa, then been ground, then it had a long journey on a big boat to our country, got packaged and then sent to a supermarket. So thank you, Lord, for coffee. Amen.

Lord, thank you for the night which has safely passed, and the beginning of another day which I shall try to use in your service. I have no way of knowing what this day will bring, but if news should be good I shall thank you, and if it should be bad then I shall ask for your help. Whatsoever shall come to pass, let me think of others rather than myself. Amen.

I pray for your healing power in our lives. Guard our thoughts, our hearts, our words, and help us to see each other as your children.
Amen.

Prayers for use at a quiet moment

Lord, help me get the right perspective on things. It's easy to get confused and distracted, so help me see clearly the true value of what really matters to you with my family and friends.

Lord, help me to be more like you.

Lord, we thank you for the richness and variety of life, and for the challenges and opportunities it brings. May each new experience teach us something more about your world and our place in it, and help us to grow more worthy to be your children. Amen.

Lord, help us to recognize what is important in life. Help us to see the simple truths which you have taught us, about how to live, and how to love one another; and show us how to apply them to the complicated world in which we find ourselves.

If I am still,
    and listen carefully
I can hear God's voice
    in the wind which rustles
      through the leaves of the trees.
If I am still,
    I can find God
    in the scent of a rose.
If I am still,
    I can see God
    in the glory of a sunset.
O Lord, teach me to be still.

Prayers for use
with the children at teatime

You might like to use a candle as you say or one or more of these prayers. One member of the family may light it, and another blow it out at the end.

Dear Lord, please help us all to grow closer to you and always remember to share your love with others. Amen.

Dear God, thank you for rain and sun
and for my mom and dad. Amen.

Dear God, thank you for my mom and dad.
Thank you for putting me on earth.
Thank you for the food I eat.
I'm sorry for the times I'm bad and
do things I shouldn't.
Amen.

Dear God, thank you for my pets.
Thank you that I can love them
and look after them.
Thank you for our wonderful world with
all the strange and beautiful animals.
Help people to protect them and stop
them being killed.
Amen.

MOM:

Let's keep quiet in God's company.
Think back over today,
and say sorry for what's been wrong.

  Pause and talk about it.

Say thank you for all that's happened to us.

  Pause and talk about it.

SON OR DAUGHTER:

Night falls, but God's light still shines.

ALL:

The light shines from God's loving face,
the light that brings us happiness,
the light we see in Jesus Christ.
As darkness fills the sky above,
we praise God's everlasting love,
the love we see in Jesus Christ.

Father God,
thank you that you are always with us.
Help us to understand that you never leave us;
your presence is always there,
even though we cannot see you.
Amen.

Father God, thank you for giving us our mothers
and fathers, our grandparents, our brothers and
sisters, our teachers and friends. Thank you for
giving us one another, that we may love as you
love us. Amen.

Dear God,
thank you for our families who we love, and who
love us. Thank you for our friends at school who
help and encourage us.
Amen.

Dear God,
thank you for our teachers, our mom and dad,
our sisters and brothers, and our pets,
and help us to be better behaved.
Amen.

Prayers for use before a meal

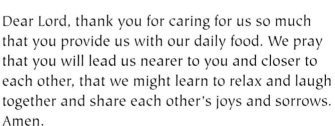

Thank you for this food. Amen.

For what we are about to receive
may the Lord make us truly grateful.
Amen.

For every cup and plateful
may the Lord make us truly grateful.
Amen.

Dear Lord, thank you for caring for us so much
that you provide us with our daily food. We pray
that you will lead us nearer to you and closer to
each other, that we might learn to relax and laugh
together and share each other's joys and sorrows.
Amen.

O God,
to those who have hunger give bread,
to those who have bread give a hunger for justice.
Amen.

For good food and good friends, thank you.
Amen.

Dear God,
Thank you for bananas, apples, and oranges.
Thank you for cake, cheese and chocolate.
Thank you for chips, doughnuts and hot dogs.
Thank you for ice cream!

Prayers for use at the end of the day

Dear God, Thank you for a lovely day.
I'm really looking forward to tomorrow.
Amen.

The sun goes down at 8 o'clock.
The moon comes up behind the dock.
The children rest their sleepy heads,
Thank you, God, for our warm beds. Amen.

Dear Father, we praise you for all the beautiful things we have seen today, and the things we have enjoyed doing: for the talking with people we have met, and for the whistling and singing when we are happy. We thank you, Lord, for our mouths. Help us to use them to praise you. For Jesus' sake. Amen.

MOM OR DAD:

Let's listen to what God tells us in the Bible.

> *Read a short passage from the Bible. It may be the next paragraph of the Bible passage you are reading, or if you have a children's Bible read one of its adapted stories.*

SON OR DAUGHTER:

It's time to remember how God has led and helped us!

> *Pause and talk about what has happened during the day.*

It's time to think about people who need praying for!

> *Pause and talk about who we want to pray for tonight, naming people or situations as an act of prayer.*

MOM OR DAD:

Let's say together the Lord's Prayer:
Our Father...

> *All join in.*

ALL:

Shine in our darkness, Father; keep us safe through the night, and wake us up ready to meet you in another day. For Jesus Christ's sake. Amen.

O Lord,
we praise you for our eyes and all that
we have seen today, through your gift of light.
We thank you for all the changes in the sky,
from the pale light of morning to the diamond
spangled velvet of night. We thank you for all
the people who have smiled at us today.
Amen.

Thank you for all the varied sounds
we have heard today: friendly voices,
beautiful music, happy laughter, birds singing,
cats purring, trains rumbling, aircraft flying over
– for so many different things,
we praise you, Lord. Amen.

Thank you, Lord, for our feet. They have taken us
all to different places, to do different things today.
They've given us plenty of fun and excitement too
– football, dancing and playing games. Thank
you for the freedom we have because of our feet.
Amen.

As we draw to the close of this day,
May you enfold us with your love,
That your abiding presence may be ever near.
Thank you for your constant watch over us,
And may you send your angels to be with us
through the night. Amen.

Lord, the children have gone to bed,
I've finished the phone calls I needed to make,
the toys are put away and I've cleared up
the kitchen. I may not have changed
the world and I have not been perfect,
but I've done a pretty good job with the
responsibilities you have given me today.
So thanks.

Two evening hymns to use on a special occasion
or when there's a bit more time. In the first, you might
divide up the verses for different voices.

My breath, my heart, my mind,
     my whole life fills with joy
because of God, who's not forgotten me,
     whose strength surrounds and lifts me up.
All through the centuries that have passed
     God showed his patience and forgiveness;
God makes the proud and pompous folk look
     foolish,
     and cares for the simple ones who trust him.
God turns the rich and selfish into beggars.
     God feeds the hungry and the poor.
All through the centuries, God is faithful
     to those he promises will be his friends.
Your beauty fills the earth and the sky;
     the saints and angels sing to you;
God everlasting, Father, Son and Holy Spirit.

(Adapted from Luke 1)

Time to let go.
We've heard your promise and now we've seen
   what you can do.
We've seen how you act to rescue your people,
   how your actions give light in a dark,
      doubtful world.
We know that we can trust you;
   time to let us go and rest.

Your beauty fills the earth and the sky;
   the saints and angels sing to you;
God everlasting, Father, Son and Holy Spirit.

(Adapted from Luke 2)

Prayers for use at special times of the year

for a birthday

*In the morning, at the end of
the usual morning prayers:*

MOM OR DAD:

Thank you, God, for giving us *(name of the
birthday boy/girl)* as part of our family.
Thank you for another year in *his/her* life.
Thank you that the more we grow, the
more we can find out about you. Keep us
growing and learning – and give us a happy
day to celebrate! Amen.

BIRTHDAY BOY/GIRL:

Thank you, God, for friends and presents and
parties. Help me remember that all happiness
comes from you; you are the most exciting gift
of all. Amen.

In the evening before bed, at the beginning
of the usual evening prayers:

Birthday boy/girl:
Thank you for the chance to enjoy my birthday.
Thank you for the year that's gone by. I promise
to do all I can to live close to you in the year
ahead, when things are easy and when things are
difficult, because I know you've promised to be
close to me and be there for me every day. Amen.

for Christmas Eve

Mom or Dad:
This is such an exciting time, it's hard to be
quiet. But let's keep quiet for a moment in
God's company. Let's remember the greatest
Christmas present of all.

Someone reads Isaiah 9.6.

You might like to sing a carol at this point.

A candle is lit.

Son or daughter:
The light shines from God's loving face,
The light that brings us happiness,
The light we see in Jesus Christ.

As darkness fills the sky above,
We praise God's everlasting love,
The love we see in Jesus Christ.

Mom or Dad:
God's Son was born on earth.
The light of God filled him and the darkness
couldn't swallow it up.

Thank you, God, for this most
wonderful of times. You've given
us all the love you can give.
Help us to pass the light of love
on to others and become
Christmas presents to them.
Amen.

MOM OR DAD:

Let's say together the Lord's Prayer:
Our Father …

All join in.

ALL:

Dear God, you make us glad every
year as we remember the birth of Jesus.
May the Holy Spirit give us such love
and thankfulness that we may long to
meet Jesus everywhere and in everyone,
in earth and in heaven.
Amen.

for Good Friday, *preferably in the morning*

SON OR DAUGHTER:

Today Jesus died because the world was too greedy and selfish and frightened to listen to him. Let's think about the times we've been greedy and selfish and frightened ...

MOM OR DAD:

But today we learn that nothing we do, however terrible, can stop God loving us.

> Short reading, such as Isaiah 53.4-5, Luke 23.33-34a, or Romans 8.38-39.

> Hymn or song, such as 'There is a green hill', 'Praise to the holiest', 'Here is love, wide as the ocean'.

SON OR DAUGHTER:

Dear Jesus, there isn't much anyone can say today. We know the world is in such a state that human beings don't know how to receive the love you give them. We're so sorry for all we do that keeps the world in a mess. But thank you for promising that neither you nor your Father in heaven will ever turn us away. Amen.

for the Easter season

Don't forget to put in as many 'Alleluias' as you like at the beginning and end of the usual morning and evening prayers!

At the start of breakfast prayers:

Jesus has been raised from the dead.
He trampled under his feet all that keeps us apart from God. He has given new life to all the world.
Alleluia!

At the start of teatime and bedtime prayers:

God brought Jesus back from death and gave us the Holy Spirit so that we may be more alive than ever. Alleluia!

for Harvest

Thank you, Lord, for all you have given us.
Warm, safe homes, a plentiful land and all of
our comforts in life. Let us remember that not
all people are as lucky as we are: people are
homeless, poor and hungry. Thank you for the
good harvest we have had, and the supplies of
fresh water we enjoy. Harvest time reminds us of
all the many things that we have to be grateful
for. Amen.

Thank you for sending us a good harvest.
We are very grateful. We recognize that we have
so much while others have so little, so help us to
be mindful of the needs of others and give
generously to those in need. Amen.

Lord, help us to realize how lucky we are to have
a plate of food in front of us. So for those who
grew it, sold it and cooked it, we say thank you.
Amen.

Dear God, thank you for the good food we eat
and all the good things we have. Thank you for
the water we have to drink. Thank you for our
families, our parents, sisters, brothers and
friends. Thank you for our homes. For all your
good gifts, we say thank you. Amen.

Prayers when we are grateful for our friends

Lord, I thank you for my friends.
When I am confused, they give me wisdom.
When I feel sad, they help me smile.
When I feel worthless, they share their love.
Lord, above all this, I thank you that you are
my friend for ever. Amen.

Dear God, thank you for our friends. We will
take care of them all and give them help when
they need it most. Help us to stick together
and never break up. You are like a friend as
well, so we will try not to leave anyone out.
Help us to apologize when we have had an
argument. Amen.

Dear God, thank you for my friends who are
there for me when I'm lonely. They are kind
and loving. They always know how I feel.
They make me laugh when I don't feel well,
and when I'm happy they make me smile
from ear to ear. Even when they get cross
with me, I know inside they still like me.
Amen.

Dear God,
thank you for our friends,
the people we like and who play with us.
Please bless them and care for them. Amen.

Dear Lord, we thank you for our friends. Not just
school friends and work friends, but our family –
we value them all. Without our friends we would
be sad, lonely and unhappy, so I say thank you.
Amen.

Lord, I pray that you will watch over all my family
and my friends wherever they may be – in this
world and the next. I pray especially for my wife,
and I give thanks for many happy years together.
I pray also for our children and their families. I
remember those who have fallen on hard times,
and ask for strength to help them in any way that
I can. I ask in the name of Jesus Christ. Amen.

Prayers when we appreciate our families

Thank you for the blessing of my wonderful
family. Please God, help all those families who
are experiencing difficulties and problems.

Dear Lord,
thank you for our families, who love us.
Even when we get mad with each other we
still love each other. Thank you for our families,
who feed us and tidy up our rooms, and we
should repay them by doing some housework
as well. Thank you for our families, who cook
our food and try their hardest to keep a roof
over our heads. Amen.

Thank you, God, for our mommies,
    who love us very much.
Thank you, God, for our daddies,
    who take care of us.
Thank you, God, for our brothers and sisters,
    who share things with us.
Thank you, God, for our friends, who help us.
Thank you for all our friends and families.
Amen.

Dear God, thank you for my family and friends,
who help me when I need them. Please help me
to respect them and to help them as well. Amen.

Lord, sometimes the world is such a hard place to
be. People can be unkind, hurtful and seek to tear
us down. As a family, Lord, help us to love and
support one another, and to never, ever add to the
hurtfulness that surrounds us, even though we're
tempted. Amen.

Lord, help us as a family to join together as a
solid wall, sheltering one another in times of
trouble. May we recognize the incredible gift we
have in each other and guard it fiercely. Be with
us when we fail each other and help us to mend
our wall so that we can stand strong. Amen.

Thank you for my mom and dad.
I realize how lucky I am to have both of them.
Amen.

Dear God, thank you for the love of our families,
our moms and dads, grannies and grandads.
Amen.

Dear Lord, bring peace and love to our families
and to families throughout the world. Amen.

Prayers when our families drive us mad

Lord, I wish I was more patient, but my family can make me so mad at times. Help me to remain calm and not get so emotional. Give me the strength not to react before counting to ten. Amen.

Dear Lord, please help me to forgive my brother. Amen.

Dear Lord, we thank you for our families who sometimes drive us crazy, but only through love. Help us to understand this, and not to think that they don't love us. Help us not to take them for granted. Amen.

Dear Lord, please help us to love our friends and families. Amen.

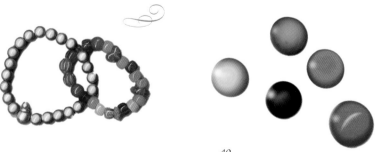

Prayers when we are unsure of the future

Lord, help us to know your will for our lives,
and have the courage to accept it. Amen.

Lord, please be with us. Help us always to have
faith in you and not to be afraid. Amen.

Lord, I am cold.
I am lonely and afraid.
Put out your hand
and grasp mine,
so that I may feel
your comforting warmth.
Keep me safe,
so that my hammering heart
may know your stillness
now and for ever. Amen.

Lord, take my hand and lead the way. Amen.

Father, when I am lost and lose sight of you,
when I forget my prayers and I'm swept away
with life and all its difficulties, when I'm too busy
and you get shoved to the bottom of the pile,
remind me that all I have to do is stop!
For I know that you will find me and be with me,
wherever I am. Amen.

Dear God, help us to see change as an exciting
new adventure, rather than a big worry.
Keep us safe travelling on our own; help us cope
with new subjects and extra homework.
Help us find our way around. Let us not be scared
of the bigger and much older pupils. Give us the
sense not to give in to pressure to do things that
we know are wrong. Help us to think of change as
a new beginning. Amen.

43

rayers when we are thinking of our church and community

We pray for all those who are persecuted for their faith. Give them strength and courage to hold on to what they know to be good and true. Amen.

Heavenly Father, we pray that your church may be continually led by your Spirit. Fill us to overflowing with the power of your love, so that we may show your practical concern for those who are our friends and neighbours. Amen.

Dear Lord,
bless all who believe in you and
help them to strengthen their faith.
Amen.

Lord, we thank you for our church leaders, and
for all their commitment in trying to bring the
message of your love to our community. Give
them greater wisdom, faith and love and fill them
with your Holy Spirit to do your will. Amen.

Lord Jesus, we pray for the young people in our
church, that they may have the courage to be
strong in faith. Amen.

Prayers when
we feel unloved, lonely or different

Lord, you know when I feel lonely and
discouraged. Please help me to realize that I do
not need to seek your presence, but that I am
living in it daily and can never be alone. Amen.

Lord, I feel lonely and unloved by everyone.
Help me to realize that your love is everlasting
and will never leave me. Help me also to feel your
presence, so that I can come through this hard
time with your help. Amen.

Dear Lord, there are times in our
lives when we feel lonely and
depressed. Guide us through these
dark times in our lives. When we
are low, remind us of that special
love you have for all of us.
You love us so much that you
died for us.
Help us to remember this, and to
know that you will always be
with us, whatever happens in
our lives. Amen.

Prayers when we are concerned for our world and the environment

Dear Lord, bring peace to the whole world. Amen.

Lord, give strength to broken lives, relationships, and communities, in Jesus' name. Amen.

I pray for the end of suffering of the innocent throughout the world. Amen.

Lord, please help people who live in countries where there is war, where families have been split up, and where the land has been devastated; where people don't dare leave the shelter of their homes because of the risk of landmines, and where food is scarce. Amen.

O Lord, our heavenly Father,
  we pray for peace on earth
  and for goodwill between all humankind,
  and wherever there is still fighting,
  help them to settle all their differences
  by peaceful negotiations.
Bless those working to relieve the suffering
  caused by the fighting;
  keep them all safe from every danger.
Amen.

Lord,
Be near us.
Be close to us.
Give us your peace.
Give us your healing.
Give us your strength.
Come soon in glory,
and heal the world.
Amen.

Dear God,
Help us to make the earth a better place.
Help us to stop polluting the air, water and soil.
Help us to recycle more and keep the earth
    tidy.
Help us not to litter the countryside but
    keep it clean.
Help us to keep our earth a
    nicer place.
    Amen.

Prayers when there have been misunderstandings

Dear Lord,
please help me to be more understanding
and caring for others.
Amen.

Lord Jesus, give us grace and sensitivity to reassure each member of the family that they are loved and valued. Help us to overcome our fears and anxieties, and strengthen our resolve to live in peace. Amen.

Lord, I cannot understand how on earth what I said seems to have been so misunderstood. I knew perfectly well what I meant, but they have interpreted things from a completely different perspective. Lord, things are a mess. Help me to have enough humility and good grace to work through this problem. Amen.

Dear God, I forgot. I know I don't have a perfect memory, but I forgot to tell them and now they are really upset. I failed to appreciate fully how important this was to them and to give it a higher priority. As a result there is this really bad atmosphere between us. Lord, help me to apologize and rebuild our relationship. Amen.

Prayers when we are stressed

Dear Lord, I am finding life hard and frustrating; nothing seems to work out right. I pray that your love and strength will sustain me through this time, and that your Spirit will guide me so that I become aware of your will, and fulfil it to the best of my ability. Amen.

Lord, there is never enough time. Not enough time for my marriage, for my kids, my work and all that I have to do. At times I feel as if I'm just surviving. I feel as if I'm barely holding on, but what I do feel is that you need to hold on to me. Amen.

Lord, the children had us up last night yet again. A decent night's sleep seems a distant memory. We are all getting tired and irritable with each other. Help us to get through this difficult time without getting too stressed out. Amen.

Dear Lord, please help us as we go through this difficult time together as a family. Help us to be open to one another, and may this time of sadness and uncertainty bring us closer together. We pray that we may walk through united and come out stronger, more loving, and with good stories to tell of how you have helped us. Amen.

Lord,
why is life such an endless rush?

Prayers when
we want to say sorry

Dear Lord, please forgive me when I've been rude or impatient with others. I've been too focused on myself, and lacking in understanding for others. I'm sorry. Amen.

Thank you, heavenly Father, that when we are truly sorry and repent of our wrongdoings you remove our sins as far as the east is from the west, so great is your love and compassion. Amen.

MOM OR DAD:

Dear Lord, we are sorry for the times when we have been unkind to each other and said or done things which were selfish. Amen.

ALL:

Lord, help us to think before we speak or act and not to hurt each other. Amen.

SON OR DAUGHTER:

Lord, we are not perfect, but help us to love each other. Amen.

Prayers when we are thinking about school

Dear Lord, I don't want to go back to school.
Please make our school more fun, and I pray my
favourite football team will not get relegated.
Amen.

Dear Lord, thank you for our wonderful summer
holidays. Bless the children, the teachers and
their helpers as they all return to school. Amen.

Dear Lord, thank you for friends
and families, because no matter
what, they will always be there
and help with homework. Amen.

Dear Lord, help me to
settle in at high school.
Amen.

Dear Lord, some may be afraid of moving on
to a new school, but my belief is that we should
view the move as a chance to learn exciting and
fascinating facts that may help us in life later on.
Please help those who are afraid of moving on to
know that it is a doorway to new facts, new
friends and also that you will guide them. All they
need is your guidance and self-confidence to
achieve their goals. Amen.

Dear Father, bless our school, that working
together and playing together we may learn to
serve you and to serve one another. Amen.

Prayers when someone we know is ill

Lord, hold the hands of those suffering from long-term illness. Give strength and support to their loved ones. In the name of your son, we pray. Amen.

Dear God, we pray for Grandad, who has been ill recently. We pray that he will recover and get back to being healthy again. But if he does die, send him to a happy place where he can meet his wife again, my Grandma. Amen.

Lord, we pray for our friends who are ill. We pray for the doctors and nurses who are looking after them. Please help them to get better soon. Amen.

Prayers when someone we know has died

Lord, we cannot believe what has happened. There is an unreality about our friend's death, because he was here with us and now he has gone, never to return. Help us to come to terms with this awful tragedy, because it is to you that we look for comfort and support. Lord, help us now and give us your peace and hope. Amen.

Dear Lord, everybody is sorry for the people we love who have passed away. My Grandma died a few years ago. Please help everyone who has lost someone in their family, and help them to get over the loss. Amen.

Lord, the pain and emptiness is at times too much
to bear. My tears are triggered by the simple
memories of the one I love who is no longer here.
Give me the help I need to accept what I cannot
change, and what is so difficult to come to terms
with. Amen.

Dear God, help the people who are grieving
for the loss of a loved one and need guidance.
Show them that you are with them all the time,
and that you will help them when troubles
approach. Amen.

Prayers when children are missing a parent

Lord, thank you for our moms and dads.
Most of us are fortunate to have them both.
But we pray for Dad, who is no longer
living at home.
Amen.

Lord, we are sorry that Dad has to go away
so much. Please look after him as he travels
and bring him safely home to us. Amen.

Dear God,
we feel sorry that Mommy is no longer
living here with us. Please look after her
until she comes again to visit.
Amen.

Lord, we pray for Mommy as
she looks after us, cleans the
house and goes out to work
and tries to do all the things
that Daddy used to do as well.
Amen.

Prayers when
we want to give thanks

Dear Lord, thank you for
all the good things in life.

Thank you for all your love!

Thank you for the
gift of life.

Dear God, thank you for the trees, plants and
everything you have made on earth. Amen.

Lord God, thank you for all your blessings:
for life and health, for laughter and fun,
for all our powers of mind and body,
for our homes and the love of dear ones,
for everything that is beautiful, good and true.
Above all, we thank you for giving your Son
to be our Saviour and friend.
May we always find true happiness
in obeying you, for Jesus Christ's sake.
Amen.

Lord, in this life of ours
we take so little time to stop
and say thank you.

Dear God, thank you for the sun and blue sky.
Amen.

Thank you, God, for my home.
You give me what I need.
Thank you, God, for my family,
   for my love given and received from my
      parents, brother, sister and friends.
You give me what I need.
Thank you, God, for my pets,
      for teaching me to love and care for them.
You give me what I need.
Thank you, God, for my school and for education.
You give me what I need.
Thank you, God, for my heart – for life.
You give me what I need.
Most of all, thank you for you, God.

Dear God,
thank you for love.
Amen.